A longer stroll down

Memory Lane

Volume One

compiled and written by

Tom Collins

Photographer

&

Phillip Hickey

News Editor of the Mail

This book is published by

NORTH EAST PRESS LIMITED
Registered Office: Echo House, Pennywell,
Sunderland SR4 9ER.
Tel. (0191) 534 3001

Contents   *page*

A longer stroll down

Memory Lane

Let's be honest - there are only a few reasons for clambering up into dusty attics where the cobweb is king and you need eyes like a cat to see anything at all.

Moving house, searching for last winter's wellies or hoping to unearth a few prized possessions because an antiques roadshow is heading for town.

We'd lost the office wellies years back, we knew there were no antiques so we had to be moving- not house but offices.

The Mail was on the move. Moving into a glorious all-colour era and out of the building that had been home for many years. But before the bulldozers arrived there was a lot to find, file, fix and fling out.

So up in the attic went photographer Tom Collins.

His joy at what he found exceeded even a five-year-old's delight at Christmas. He emerged with glass negatives from all kinds of past events and set about printing them up almost immediately.

We watched as bygone days appeared before our eyes - an intriguing insight into Hartlepool's history. *A STROLL DOWN MEMORY LANE*.

If only there were more pictures we thought. So up Tom went and the screams of pleasure announced he had found more. Boxes and boxes more, in unbelievably good condition.

Within days we were printing them in the Mail and the response was staggering. Letters from all over the world with details of every picture and daily requests for more and more photographs.

The rest, as they say, is history.

Are you being served

HARTLEPOOL today is a virtual copy of every other town centre in Britain - the same multi- national shops selling the same goods at the same prices.

How different to a few years back when family-owned stores with personal service made shopping a pleasure.

Boiled sweets from a woman in a crisp white apron, meat from a butcher who learned the trade from his dad - and had the cut hands to show where he'd made a few mistakes.

Lynn Street was packed with shopping gems including a superb indoor market. It also had the Empire Theatre and the North-Eastern pub

Church Street, set for a new lease of life now, was home to Camerons wine store, Edgar Phillips, Kirby's Cafe and so much more. Forget your plastic palaces after quick profits, these were shops to savour.

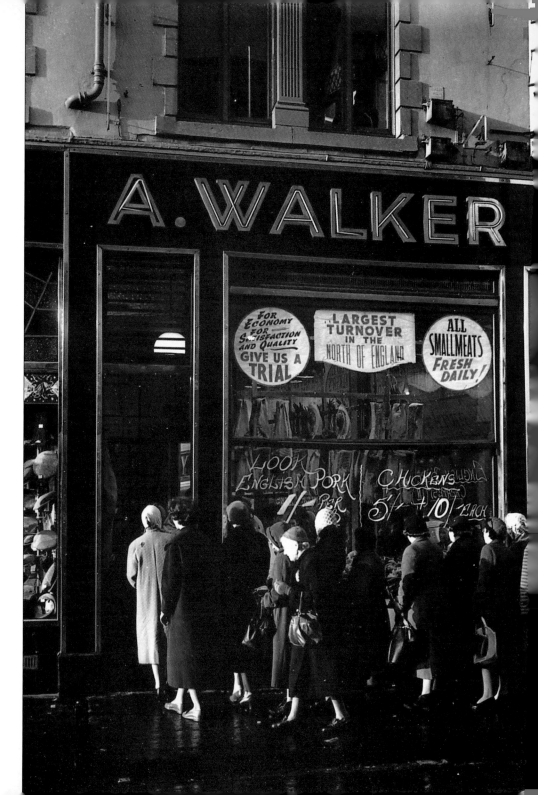

Forget the Rationing
Let's have a mix-up

5

Great Shops in Lynn Street

Lynn Street with Commercial Hotel on the left

*Disc Delights
in Bruce Moore's*

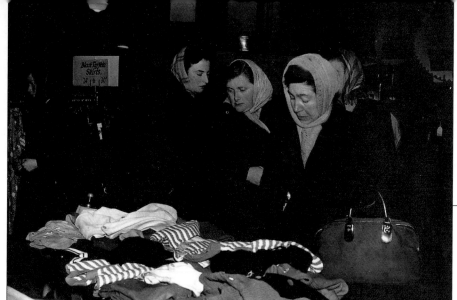

Eye for a Bargain

York Road and Junction of South Road

*Lynn
Street*

Lynn Street Showing the North Eastern and the Empire

*Northgate
Shops*

Beside the Seaside

For generations it was the only taste of the sea air they would get in a year - and the seaside fish and chips.

Seaton Carew was a real British resort, thousands flocked there when the sun appeared. Not just from Hartlepool but from the pit villages, Stockton and Middlesbrough - with the added thrill for the Boro families of a crossing on the Transporter.

The prom was lined with ice-cream covered kids, the beach packed with young women in what were then considered daring costumes - and men who refused to even take off their flat caps.

Fed-up with Seaton? Then take a dip in the paddling pool at the Headland or bask on the Fish Sands, if you could find a few spare feet of beach as entire families took picnics and pushchairs and settled down for the day.

Wherever you chose, there was a great day out for everyone in those days when we had real summers and we knew how to enjoy them.

Jumping for Joy

Seaton . . . But keep your caps on!

LF

Collins Fairground.
What a scream

Queueing for
Deck Chairs
at Seaton

A stroll at
Seaton

Seaton Beauties . . .
where are they now?

Have a splashing time

Seaton shopkeepers would love these scenes today

14

Lovely legs lads.
The old paddling pool on the headland

15

The fish sands again.
Get there early.

17

Fish and Ships

Hartlepool would probably never have survived but for it's links with the sea.

Even today, it's regeneration is being built on the sea with the new marina forming the back-bone of the bid to bring the good times back to the town.

Shipbuilding and fishing employed thousands. Sons followed their fathers into the industries, they were not just jobs but ways of life.

Goods were imported and exported to and from almost every port in the world. Timber came in, coal went out with strong-arm dockers doing much of the work by hand.

The fishing fleet still exists but is a shadow of what it used to be. The Fish Quay was a mini-village in itself, men mending nets, some filleting and others repairing boats.

Great characters with amazing names who are still talked about in the pubs down there today.

Slippery customers. . . characters from the fish sands

19

Super ships in Hartlepool

TRENTWOOD
MIDDLESBOROUGH

A tug owned by the Railway Company

Timber!!
Loads of it.

The mothballed Royal Navy Fleet

Football Crazy

Even Stanley Matthews emerged from the attic when we dusted down the collection of forgotten negatives.

Playing at Ayresome Park and in classic Matthews pose - jinking past defenders as fans home and away looked on in admiration.

Closer to home there are pictures of the good old days - were they really any different - at the Victoria Ground.

Some amazing queues for the big games of the past, probably Manchester United, and scenes every ageing football fan will remember of pitches waterlogged or covered in snow.

And what about the womens' teams, they caused quite a stir in the town and certainly looked happy playing the game.

Grim Faces!
Good Players?

*Get in. Yes, a goal
at the Victoria Ground*

28

*Come on Pools... or was
it Chelsea visiting
the town?*

29

Going: A bit soft

*Pools' own
snowmen*

*Long time since Pools
saw crowds like this*

*Sir Stanley Matthews
at Ayresome Park*

On Parade

Hardly an occasion big or small was allowed to pass in Hartlepool without someone organising a parade to mark it.

And once the parade was organised, thousands of people used to go along.

They became great events in the town and the Mail was there to record them - from military marches to womens' groups and carnivals.

The streets were always lined with children enthralled by the spectacle of people marching in step or holding colourful banners or marching silently.

Give Hartlepool something to celebrate and they did it in style.

Stepping out on York Rd.

Even the ladies loved to march

Military men march past Binns and the old library

Church Street

Headland Carnival

Jazzing up the Headland

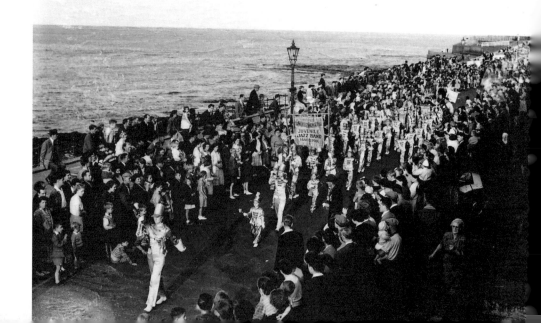

Little Angels...weren't they?

Teddy Gardiner

HARTLEPOOL has had some sporting legends over the years - but few greater than Teddy Gardner.

Known as the Hartlepool Box 'O Tricks - weren't boxers nicknames so much better then - Gardner started his professional career at the amazing age of just 12 years old in 1934.

His most famous fight was against Jackie Patterson, the British and Empire bantamweight champion in 1948 - at West Hartlepool Greyhound Stadium.

He won on a narrow points decision and went on to win the European flyweight title in February 1952 and the British title in the following month.

Thousands of people followed his fights through the pages of Mail and many people still talk about him today as Hartlepool's greatest ever boxer.

Here we go

Teddy in Action

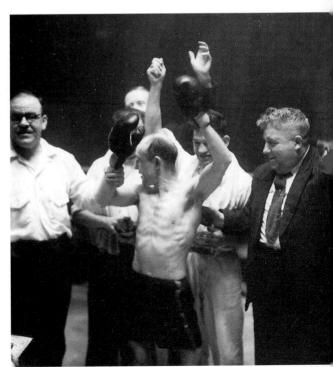

I name this ship

Whatever new age industries come to Hartlepool, the town will always be linked with shipbuilding.

Up to 10 ships a year were being built in the town in the 1950s, showing off the incredible skills of Hartlepool craftsmen to the whole world.

The Silverburn launched in 1952 with a deadweight of 8,850 tonnes, the Atlantic Countess, owned by Atlantic Freighters, launched in 1954, and the Perang launched in the same year for Elder Dempster Lines, were just three of the vessels launched in a blaze of glory from Gray's yard.

Every launch was a grand occasion, shipbuilders and schoolchildren joining up with civic dignatories for the unforgettable moment when the ship plunged down the slipway and into the water.

All gone now. But the skills live on in the restoration of the Warrior and other vessels that have been returned to their former glory by the craftmanship of Hartlepool's legendary workforce.

*Another one
complete*

Gone forever . . . the days of shipbuilding

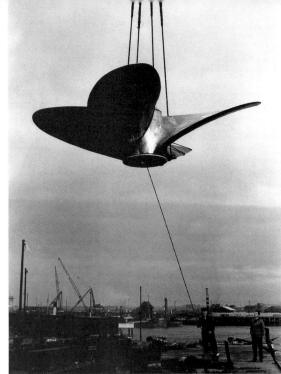

Take a last look at a dead industry

The Sporting Life

Rugby was and still is immensely popular in Hartlepool with no town in England able to boast as many people playing the game every week.

The years gone by saw a succession of players win international caps and their progress was followed avidly through the sports pages of the Mail.

A cap for a Hartlepool lad was an occasion for every sports lover in the town to celebrate.

For those less energetic, there have always been alternatives - superb golf courses and any number of bowling greens.

It's not long before a visit to a pub these days quickly turns to Hartlepool's proud sporting past – and the traditional rugby row over which was the best club, Rovers or West.

Better to stay neutral, we reckon.

Sporting Gents

Golfing ladies show great style

Rugby . . .
at the Greyhound stadium
of all places

When we were young

Were the summers really sunnier, the ice cream really tastier and the people really friendlier?

Well these photographs certainly make life look a lot happier and less stressful than it is now.

Just look at the smiles on the faces of all the children.

Even crossing the road seemed to give them something to laugh about.

There'll be people buying this book suddenly seeing themselves in a picture for the first time in years and thinking....THEY WERE THE DAYS.

Amazing memory. All elephants have them.

All dressed up with somewhere to go

49

*Pretty patriots
and their Union Jacks*

St Cuthberts kids cross Brenda Rd

51

Not happy with his rations

Hard work harvesting

Horses at the Wesley
Now it's Cats and Rats

Pigeon Men
Ready for Racing

Great to be out. Steelworkers ride away from Number One Mill

Yes missus, we'll be back with your eggs soon

Who left that lamp post there?

Anyone got a tow rope?

Out of Africa – into Hartlepool

Carnival Capers

Leaving on a Plane . . . not a Jet!

Greatham Airport

Big Brother's Watching you

61

Subscribers

Sir Richard Storey, Bt.

Michael Kearney

Charles D. Brims

Gerry Kenny

Stuart D. Bell

Councillor Gladys Worthy, Mayor of Hartlepool

Andrew G. Hughes

Rita Shenton

Adrian Martin

Edmund Redshaw

Stephen Gascoigne

Tommy Cram

Keith Metcalfe

Keith Fergus

Paul C. James

Edmund & Joyce Smith

Diana H. Comber

Alan Robinson

Russel Warnock

Eva Flangan

Subscribers

Aileen Woolston	Brian Burnitt
Ian John Flounders	Alistair & Kathleen McKie
William Doyle	Sara Branfoot
Charles Sidney West	John Branfoot
Bridget McKenzie	Joan Proud
Alexander Francis	Jean Taylorson
William Melvin Carter	Patricia Mary Betson
Eddie Robinson	John Hajdasz
Nora Sutherst	Sheila Stoneman (née Stout)
Cynthia Margaret Sutherst	Sengelow Family
Derek Hodgson	Pladdys Family
Ann Ellen Wilkinson	Davies Family